# INVESTIGATING THE KENSINGTON RUNE STONE AND ITS AUTHENTICITY

## By:

## Austin A. Mardon

## By Austin Mardon

Who's Who in Federal Politics from Alberta Ridings 1972;
English Studies at Canadian Universities 1972;
Community Names of Alberta 1975
By Austin Mardon & Ernest Mardon
Alberta Judicial Biographical Dictionary 1990;
Alberta Ethnic Mormon Politicians 1991;
Alberta Ethnic German Politicians 1991;
When Kitty Met the Ghost 1991;
Down & Out & On the Run in Moscow 1991;
The Girl Who Could Walk Through Walls 1991;
Alberta Mormon Politicians 1992;
Alberta General Election Returns & Subsequent Byelections
1882-1992 1993;
Edmonton Political Biography 1994;
Alberta Political Biographical Dictionary 1994;
Alberta Executive Council 1905-1990 1994;
Early Christian Saints 1997;
Later Christian Saints for Children 1997;
Many Christian Saints for Children 1997;
Childhood Memories & Legends of Christmas Past 1998;
Community Names of Alberta 1999;
Men of Dawn 1999;
United Farmers of Alberta 1999;
The Genealogy of the Mardon Family 2000;
Alberta Catholic Politicians 2000; Alberta Anglican Politicians
2001;
Liberal Politicians in Alberta 1905-1992 2002;
What's in a Name? 2002;
Edmonton Members of the Legislature 2004;
Senators and Members of the House of Commons from
Edmonton
Edmonton Municipal Politicians 2005;
Alberta Francophone Politicians 2007.

# INVESTIGATING THE KENSINGTON RUNE STONE AND OTHER ESSAYS

By:

## Austin Albert Mardon

## Catherine Mardon

Edited By:

## Aala Abdullahi

## Golden Meteorite Press

A Golden Meteorite Press Book.

© 2011 copyright by Austin Mardon, Edmonton, Canada.

Cover design Aala Abdullahi, 2011

Published by Golden Meteorite Press.
126 Kingsway Garden
Post Office Box 34181,
Edmonton, Alberta, CANADA.
T5G 3G4
Telephone: +1-780-378-0063
Email: aamardon@yahoo.ca
Web site: www.austinmardon.org
**ISBN** 978-1-897472-27-9

Library and Archives Canada Cataloguing in Publication
Mardon, Austin A. (Austin Albert)

    Investigating the Kensington Rune Stone and its authenticity
/ Austin Albert Mardon.

Includes bibliographical references.
ISBN 978-1-897472-27-9

    1. Kensington Rune Stone.  I. Title.

E105.M36 2011          977.6'45          C2011-904437-4

Dedicated

to

Catherine Mardon

# Table of Contents

Description of the Stone:

It is 36 inches long, 15 inches wide, five and a half inches thick and weighs 230 pounds.

When found on Olaf Ohman's farm in Douglas County, Minnesota, November 1898, it was face down entangled in the roots of a popular tree,

## I. THE KENSINGTON STONE

The case of Kensington Stone is most interesting. Personally, I am not yet convinced that it is a forgery or a hoax. First, let us look at the accepted authentic Kingistorssuaq rune stone which was discovered on the Greenland west coast above the Arctic Circle in 1824. Archaeologists and historians agree on the authenticity of this rune stone that lists the names of Norse men and the date at which they reached this point near Upernavik. The find was made by the Eskimo Pelimut just short of latitude 73 degrees North in the high Arctic. The runic inscription states that in the year 1333 that three Norse Greenlanders had camped and spent the winter at Kingigtorisuaq. The runic script was still in use in Scandinavia at this time, mostly for inscriptions on tombstones.

Since then, three cairns, thought to have been of Greenland Norse origin, have been discovered in the high Canadian Arctic- one at Jones Sound in latitude 76 degrees 35" North, and a further two on Washington Irving Island in latitude 79 degrees North. The inhospitable nature of the terrain may have discouraged permanent Norse settlements.

Ohman and his fellow settlers were serious, hard working and honest. They were all practicing members of the Lutheran Protestant Church. They were sober, god-fearing pioneer settlers. It was not easy

3

work to clear the stumps and drain the marshy land for the plough. (Personal Observation: My grandfather, the late Austin Mardon, after being seriously wounded in German East Africa early in World War I, spent three winters working on a farm near Black Duck, Minnesota. He had the greatest respect for his melancholic Scandinavian neighbors, and used to say it would be "out of character" for them to play a hoax. He used to say his neighbors believe the Kensington Stone was authentic.)

Ohman could not even make out what the language was, and gave it to a friend, J.P. Hedberg, who helped settlers bring their families out from the old country. Hedberg wrote to the editor of Svenska Amerikanska Poster, a Swedish weekly newspaper published in Minneapolis. He said "the inscription appeared to be in old Greek letters." (See: letter from J.P. Hedberg to Swan Turnblad, dated January., 1899 quoted in Holand, P. 163.)

From this letter, it would appear that Hedberg was not a scholar and an indifferent speller. The runic alphabet, the Futhark, looks to the casual reader similar to the Classic Greek alphabet.

The editor, Swan J. Turnbald, was unfamiliar with the Futhark, and in the Feburary 28, 1899 issue of Svenska Americanska Posten published both Hedberg's letter and a copy of the original inscription.

Meanwhile S.A. Sieverts, the Swedish bank manager in Kensington, wrote to Professor O.J. Breda, head of the Scandinavian Language Department at the University of Minnesota. Professor Breda was the first individual to recognize this care-worn stone as containing a runic inscription. As one of the most influential academic Scandinavian scholars in the State, it is worth noting that professor Brdea could only translate the inscription in part. He was unfamiliar with fourteen letters and all of the seven numbers used.

If the Kensington stone is a forgery, who would have the knowledge of the Futhark to carve it in Minnesota of the 1890's?

R. Donald Logan, a professor at Boston's Emmanuel College in 1893, maintained it was a forgery, carved by a person having some knowledge of the runic alphabet and familiarity with the peculiar Norwegian/Swedish local dialect.

If this person ever did exist, he knew not some by had a great deal of knowledge of the Futhark, in fact, be a great runic scholar that knew more than the head of Scandinavian Language Department and his colleagues. He would also have to know the numeral system used in runic inscription. He would also have to understand the late Medieval devotion to the Blessed Virgin Mary. It is questionable whether a 19th century Lutheran homesteader or Lutheran priest would include any reference to the Blessed Virgin Mary.

The fact that the unknown carver was runic letters familiar among the Swedes or Goths, and the

Norse or Norwegian could be explained by reference to the text. The opening phrase indicates

"(We are) '8 Goths and 22 Norsemen.' "

Turning to the use of runes, it was the 'national' script of the ancient North German peoples. The origin of the runic alphabet still remains uncertain. I have an original hypothesis that I shall expand upon in a future paper.

In passing, I would like to draw attention to Logan's mistranslation of "A V M", it is usually rendered as 'Ave Virgo Maria', or "Hail Virgin Mary', not as he does 'Ave Maria'.

Runes were mainly a monumental script as it is used on the Kensington stone. After the Vikings became Christians in the 11th Century, the use of runes decline. However, we have the Kingigtorssuaq stone carved by Greenland Norse at about the same time as it is alleged the Kensington stone was carved "somewhere" in continental America.

The mixture of Nordic and Gothic runes, and even the archaic runes, were not in use in Europe at the time; maybe this was because the Vinland explorers had come from the remote and isolated occidental Greenland colony. The fact, if a runic expert were to produce a forged inscription, it would lack any irregularities. He would pattern his work after a known inscription. Thus, the inclusion of the same word with different spelling is in keeping with linguistic practices in England, for example, at about this time. Let us not forget that even in the Elizabethan Age spelling and grammatical usage had not been standardized and that in official documents William Shakespeare spelt his name in 13 different ways.

Who was the carver of the Kensington stone?

If he was one of the Scandinavian Minnesota pioneer settlers, where did he receive his training? He could have had stone mason carving education in Sweden. The clearness of the cutting- so well preserved makes me uneasy. But what concerns me even more is why an ordinary individual, in a small Swedish settlement, would spend his time in practical America in producing a forgery when he could turn his talents into more financially rewarding endeavors.

If he was one of the eight Goths or 22 Norsemen; if he was one of the 30 surviving explorers who had journeyed into the interior of the Continent up the rivers and returned from a fishing expedition to find ten of their companions had been murdered, what kind of man was he? He, according to Holand, would have been a west Goth by birth. As a youth, he would have passed by and read again and again one of the 2,500 centuries old runic monuments. Here, he may have become familiar with the archaic Futhark letters that he would recall and use many years later in an alien land. He must have been well educated, possibly at some time a member of a monastic community. He was a skilled artisan, a stone carver by trade and in all likelihood a soldier or priest by profession.

He would have survived the terrible visitation, which we call the Black Death in 1348 and 1349. This plague took, away a large portion of Christendom. However, this calamity had not hardened him. There is pathos and real concern for the eternal salvation of his murdered companions, "Hail Virgin Mary--- save us from evil."

(Personal Observation: After studying the meaning of the inscription of the Kensington Stone, I am reminded of the final chapters of Sigrid Unset's Nobel Prize winning historical Novel Kristin Lavramsdatter. Set in Medieval Norway at the time of the Black Death, the work is deeply rooted in the Nordic pagan past and the vital Christian present.)

This prayer shows the Medieval Christian attitude and fears in the face of sudden unexpected violent death. His ten companions, killed by natives, had had no opportunity to confess their sins and receive the absolution of the Church. One gets the impression there was a priest in the party of Norse explorers. The carver-in-stone has made them a memorial and seem to be asking the readers of his monument to remember the souls of his companions in their prayers. (Lutherans do not believe in Purgatory, which is another argument for dating the work as a 14th century tombstone.)

Referring to the geography of the locality of the tragic place, the runic inscriber informs us that 75 miles north of the marker he was preparing, the party had a camp near two rocky islands. Or we could possibly translate the phrase as near "twin buttes". I would be interested to find out whether there are two outstanding physical features north of Kensington. The village disappeared from the Times World Atlas of 1983.

It is worth noting the Medieval Norse word "Daghrise"- loosely translated "day's journey" is a reference to a unit of distance equal to about 75 miles. The words appear twice in the inscription: one when referring to their camp, near 'Twin butte' 75 miles

11

north of the projected monument, and the second time in reference to their ship and their ten companions guarding it by the sea, which is 14 'daghrise' or one thousand and fifty miles away.

Kensington is approximately nine-hundred miles due south of the mouth of the Nelson river, on the shore of the Hudson's Bay, which we conclude was the place their voyagers left their ocean going vessel. He is exact in his statement of time and place.

"The starkness of his statement: We were out and fished one day. After we came home, found ten men, red with blood and dead." This passage is reminiscent of the Sagas. A statement of fact, no explanation and is as moving as lines from The Battle of Maldon that appears in The Anglo Saxon Chronicle.

## 2.  GEOGRAPHICAL IMPLICATIONS CONNECTED WITH THE KENSINGTON STONE

We know that Norse Greenlanders were, like their Icelandic brethren, wedded to the sea. They were fishermen and experienced navigators.

The Greenland Colonies, although in apparent decline, were still vital communities in the mid-14th century. It appears reasonable that the more venturesome member of the settlement could have sailed westward through the Hudson Strait into the Ungava Bay.

Recently, Professor Thomas L Lee(1966) has discovered a number of longhouse as well as stone implements, a piece of bone and an iron ax-head on the shore of Deception Bay. These sites may have been occupied by Norse Greenlanders and/or by Dorset Eskimos.

The Norse Greenlanders could also have pushed on into the Hudson Bay and sailed southward with no difficulty. They could have found the mouth of the Nelson river without difficulty. If the inscription on the Kensington Stone is authentic, the group left ten men and their ship while the main part of more than forty men, rowed up the Nelson river and across the 240 long lake Winnipeg. They would be going up the Red River due to south for another 250 miles they would be in the general geographical location of Douglas County, Minnesota. The Nelson River-Lake Winnipeg and the Red River is an artery that leads into the heart of the continent. There are no barriers or portages required only strong willing rowers. The explorers would not lack for food. The inscription mentions fish, along the banks of the rivers and lake, there would be a plentiful supply of wild game and in season wild rice and many different kinds of wild berries.

Compared to the dangers of Atlantic storms and the inhospitable terrain in the high Arctic islands this journey for hardy Goths and Norse mariners would not be impossible.

## 3. NUMBER OF NORSE ON THE KENSINGTON STONE EXPEDITION

A careful reading of the runic inscription of this alleged 14th century monument reveals that there is ambiguity in ascertaining the number of surviving members of the group. I believe that to be logical, we must agree that when the inscription was carved there were still alive "eight Goths and 22 Norse" for a total of thirty. To this number we must add the ten men left to guard their ship, more than a thousand miles away to the north. We must conclude that they are still on the shore of the Hudson Bay near the mouth of the Nelson River, awaiting the return of the inland party of explorers. So there are still forty men to operate the ocean going vessel that brought the group from Greenland through the Hudson Straits into the inland sea. The inscription states that ten men were left to guard the camp in Modern Douglas County, Minnesota, and all of them were massacred by hostile natives.

Other may have lost their lives while on their sea voyage or on the long river journey up the Nelson across Lake Winnipeg and up the Red River. Holand states that if the group had left the mouth of the Nelson say on June 5 and had travelled up stream by oar or sail in smaller boats, they would take about two months or more to arrive in the vicinity of "Massacre Camp" near Kensington.

In the 14th Century after a long period of milder weather before the commencement of what is known as "the small ice age", the spring might have come earlier than June 1 in Northern Manitoba.

The whole journey south would have been easier in the 14th century than today. Some 12,000 years ago, the whole region was a large glacial lake, known as Lake Agassiz. The former lake basin has the wide Red River crossing it. The volume of water and the number of lakes would have been more numerous five hundred years ago. This would have been an easy journey than many of the trips the Norse made along the rivers of easy journey than many of the trips the Norse made along the rivers of Eastern Europe in the late Medieval times.

## 4. LENGTH OF TIME TO CARVE THE RUNES

The short Kingigorssaq Stone contains only fourteen words. On the other hand, the Kensington Stone contains 218 runic letters plus three Latin script letters. This makes it one of the longest later runic inscriptions.

The individual letters were evidently carved with a sharp instrument and a hammer. Each letter is clear and distinct in outline. But the fact that the upper edge of the incised line is rough and rounded as a result of the disintegration of the stone, while the bottom of the incisions is sharp and clear shows plainly that many years must have elapsed since the runic inscription was cut (See: Geological Survey, February 25, 1952, quoted in Noland).

This rune stone, forgery or not, is a fascinating work of sculptural art. The work, on examination, reveals an artist of a highly individual style. There could have been two carvers. If the stone is the work of one man, then certainly he was ambidextrous - using both his right and his left hand to hold the chisel. The quality of work done by either hand is the same.

The carver appears to have worked quickly with sure deft strokes as if he was thoroughly familiar with working in this type of slab graywacke and was a master at cutting runes. John K Daniels, an experienced sculptor, writing in The Minneapolis star (July. 1955), states "the whole job may have taken two hours." I was surprised with this statement, but then started to think of the carving in the 500 churches of Cathedral size built in France during the 14th century.

On the back side of this runic stone are very clear markings dating from the last ice age. The portion of the stone that was underground when it was first erected appears to be more weathered than the upper portion that contains the nine rows of runic symbols. On the left hand side, half way down the stone, several of the runes have become so worn to be illegible. This part of the inscription can only be read by help of the context.

This slab of graywacke is a very hard stone. One of its characteristics is that it weather slowly.

If one believes that the Kensington Stone is authentic, one must accept that it was carved and placed as a grave marker near the bodies of the ten murdered Norse who had been part of a large expedition that penetrated into the heartland of the continent. In time, the stone fell on its face, and was covered by soil. In about 1800, a poplar started to grow on top of where the stone was lying. In time, the roots of the poplar encased the stone, and was only disturbed by Olof Ohman when he was clearing the land for the plough.

## 5. WHERE DID THE KENSINGTON NORSE EXPLORERS COME FROM?

Hjalmar R. Holand, in Exploration in America Before Columbus (1956) maintains that the Kensington Norse expedition had been originally commissioned by King Magnus of Norway and Sweden to visit Greenland to help revive Christianity.

For several reasons, I believe the Kensington expedition originated in and were manned by men from the West Colony in Greenland. The settlement was under pressure from the warlike Eskimos that were drifting down the west coast of Greenland. Contact with Europe was uncertain in the decades following the Black Death and the colony's exports of Walrus-ivory and furs were no longer in such demand. Trading from various parts of Europe had fallen into the hands of cities belonging to the Hanseatic League. But of even greater significance, the weather patterns were changing. The summers were shorter and the crops did not have time to ripen while the winters were long and colder. The ice packs became thicker and wider. Greenlanders could not circumnavigate their island home as they had done in the past.

Some scholars now believe that the 300-year old West Colony emigrated on Mass at some unknown date in the 14th century somewhere to the west or the old Vinland of Greenlander Saga. The Kensington expedition could have been an advance party. Family ties were always important in Iceland and Greenland from the days of the first arrivals. Reference to Goths and Norse in the Kensington Stone inscription may only indicate the original part of the European homeland they came from. The Colony had the resources and manpower to mount the expedition. They would have the oral tradition of previous adventurers and would have in one ocean going vessel with a company of fifty men have been able to pass through Hudson Strait and breakout into Hudson Bay. Sailing south, they like the employees of the Hudson's Bay Company three centuries later, would without undue difficulty move up the inland water ways of present day Manitoba.

I still believe my father's belief that Leif Ericson's Vinland was the southern shore of Hudson

Bay may be correct. The passage from the inscription "journey from Vinland" (where the ship and ten guards were left) "round about the West", may refer to their journey upcountry.

In 1342, Bishop Gisle Oddson of Skalhot was unjustified in saying "the inhabitants of Greenland fell voluntarily away from the true faith and the Christian religion, if my hypothesis is proved to be correct. The shock at the massacre of a quarter of the Kensington Stone expedition is real. After one has forgotten hundred of details about this unique inscription, this fact remains clear (See: Holand, p.125).

CONCLUSION

The riddle of the Kensington rune stone is still waiting to be solved to the satisfaction of many scholars: historians, archaeologists and historical geographers.

It is now accepted as fact that the Norse, whether from Scandianvia or Greenland, had substantial contacts with America in the 14th Century. For example, Erick Wahlgren, the distinguished American philologist, has had his "The Vikings in America" published this autumn (1986) in London, but the trouble with this book and others of its kind, is that there are few, if any new insights. He does not go into details about recent Norse archaeological discovery of Ugava, Labrador or Newfoundland. Wahlgren dismisses the Kensington Stone as one of the fantasies of Minnesota.

There must be a clear analysis and re-examination of all the evidence regarding this strong runic stone. Just saying it is a hoax is not enough. Hjalmar Holand, the main promoter and supporter of the Pro-Kensington Stone school for fifty years, tend to weaken his own case but he is able to marshal a large number of facts. The Anti-Kensington Stone scholars merely say it is a hoax and are maddening vague on why. I wonder how we can solve the riddle of the Kensington stone once and for all.

# BIBLIOGRAPHY

Holand, Hjalmar R. Exploration in America Before Columbus. New York, Twayne, 1956.

(Contains a full account of the discovery and controversy surrounding the Kensington rune stone)

Logan, F. Donald. The Vikings in History. Totowa, N.J: Barnes and Noble, 1983.

Wahlgren, Erik. The Vikings in America. London: Thames and Hudson, 1986.

# CALLANISH: THE ENIGMA OF THE STONES

# By:

# Austin A. Mardon

## Table of Contents

**1.** PREVIOUS ARCHAELOGICAL INVESTIGATIONS AND THEIR INDIVIDUAL FINDINGS

**2.** CLASSICAL LITERARY REFERENCES TO CALLANISH

**3.** HISTORICAL MYTHS

**4.** NORTHERN EUROPE DEVELOPMENT AND A NEW CONCEPT OF HUMAN NATURE

**5.** FOLK CUSTOMS AND FOLK TALES AND THEIR RELATION TO CALLANISH

**6.** POTENTIAL RELATIONSHIPS WITH OTHER MEGALITHIC SITES

**7.** PLACE – NAME OF THE SITE

**8.** POSSIBLE FOOD ECONOMIES

## 9. THE PALEOENVIRONMENT OF THE ISLE OF LEWIS

### I. PREVIOUS ARCHAEOLOGICAL INVESTIGATIONS AND THEIR INDIVIDUAL FINDINGS

The first reference I have found to Callanish is by Martin in 1706. He referred to them as "Ye Heathen Temple". When Martin was travelling through this area asked the local inhabitants what the local customs and traditions were concerning the stones at Tursachan as they otherwise called the area. They told him that it was once a place of worship in the times of the pagans. The rituals associated with the stones were supposed to consist of the chief Druid or their priest standing at or near the big stone in the center of the circle. The chief Druid then addressed the surrounding worshipping pagans in their heinous pagan rites. At this time Martin stated that peat covered 13 feet of the stones. When Callender reported the height of the site, he stated that the stone were twelve feet high. This means that if both figures are correct, the peat grew one foot in one hundred fifty years. This also means at the time of Martin (1706) the stones still were in the local mythology. This might also mean that references to it by locals in the 19th century have some validity as a reference to what the site meant.

I have only received the preliminary report by Henry Callender to the Society of Antiquaries of Scotland. He made another report in 1858 after he excavated the site and described the burial vault and base of the stones. One of the reasons why even the second report is in the sense that there was no site report produced on the extensive excavations conducted under Callender in the 1857-1858 seasons. Callender immediately grasps the significance of this site in terms of its relationship with astronomy. His basic observations might in the end be the only valid conclusions that can be made about this site. It is entirely possible that the debate since Callender is like "each locality indulging its own fancy" to use Callender's own wording.

The astronomical significance that Callender does link is to the polar star. This in turn is linked with the cardinal point That the position was chosen and laid down from astronomical observation, can easily be demonstrated by visiting the spot on a clear night, when it will be found that by gring the upper part of the single line of stones extending to the south to bear upon the top of the large stone in the centre of the circle, the apex of that stone coincides exactly with the pole-star; this is more readily done from the south line being on sloping ground, so that looking along the line upwards to the higher level of the centre is very much the same as taking an observation through a telescope.

(Callender, 1857. p.382)

Even though Thom's work is not exclusively on Callanish, it does use Callernish as a prime specimen.

## 2. CLASSICAL LITERACY REFERENCES TO CALLANISH

Diodorus of Sicily, writing in Greek in Book 2, Chapter 47 discusses the legendary Hyperboreans, who lived beyond the Callic Celts. He states:

There lies in the ocean an island no smaller than Sicily (Britain?). This island is situated in the north and inhabited by Hyperboreans... and the island is both fertile and productive of every crop, and since it has unusually temperate climate it produces two harvests each year.

31

Later, Diodorus says, "And there is also on the island both a magnificent sacred precinct of Appolo and a notable nature of the cruciform. according to the Callender temple which... is spherical in shape". (Is the Callanish being referred to?)

He also states, Abaris, a Hyperborea, came to Greece in ancient times. They say also that the moon, as viewed from this island, appears to be but a little distance from earth and to have upon it prominances, like those of the earth, which are visible to the eye.

Daniel Defoe, the author of Robinson Crusoe, wrote: A Journey Through Scotland (Published in 1723). This is the first comprehensive guide book of the North of Scotland. Prior to this book, Scotland, especially the Hebrides, was largely terra incognita, a little known region. This work was published within sixteen years of the Act of Union between England and Scotland. Although Defoe did not visit the Isle, Julius Gais Caesar, in his Callic War (59-51 B.C.), Book 5, Chapter 13, gives the first detailed account of the geography of Britain. His description is maily based on personal observation and is in part derived from the record of Pytheas of Marseilles, a Greek traveller who circumnavigated Britain in the 4th Century B.C. - in the time of Alexander the Great. Caesar is correct in regarding the size and shape of Britain, mentions that the Isle of Man (Mona) is between Britain and Ireland and that the Island of Ireland is half of the size of Britain. The Roman general goes on to state:

In addition, several small islands are supposed to lie close to land (Hebrides), as touching which some have written that mid-winter nights there but lasts for thirty whole days. We could discover nothing about this by inquiries.

Caesar added to this, "Nisi Certis ex ague mensuris breviaves esse quani in continenti noctes videbamus" (But by exact water measurements, we observed that the nights were shorter than on the continent).

In reference to the food economy and life style of the ancient Britains, Caesar states, "Interioves plerique frumenta non serunt, sed lacta et carne virient pellibusque sunt vestiti" (Of the invaders most do not sow corn, but live on milk and flesh and clothe themselves in skins). This can be applied to my statement on the food economy of the inhabitants of Lewis; he did make a reference to it, he states that it is unlikely "any person whose business was meer curiosity and diversion, should either be at the expense of running the risk of such a hazardous passage where there was so little worth observation to be found (p. 417).

## 3. HISTORICAL MYTHS

The basis of the validity of this section is that of the preservation of mythic structures from their time of original inception. A good case is the case of

Schlieman and his discovery and excavation of Troy. At the time of Schlieman's enterprises it was maintained that the Homeric legends were mere fictional literature. As it is today, contemporary archaeologists have specifically ignored oral traditions relating to specific sites and greater questions of the archaeological nature. Although Professor Smart maintained that in Ireland at least there was some attempt to use myths to better understand sites (Smart, 1985). This is also substantiated by the conclusions of Ireland in Prehistory. According to the authors,

Islands are notoriously conservative, encouraging the retention of older traditions and resisting the introduction of newer ones: new movements into Ireland, therefore tended to produce a more complex social environment. Almost invariably, each new wave of influence to reach Ireland is found mixed with the older, indigenous culture. (Herity and Eogan, 1977, 252)

This came along with my maternal grandmother's stories about Bonnie, Prince Charlie, and how the clan McKinnon hid him once after the battle of Culloden. This was over two centuries before she was living and she spoke of it as though it had happened yesterday. The geographical position of the Outer Hebrides is such that they are protected by the Atlantic and many dangerous tidal bores. This isolation protected them from cultural assimilation until the advent of radio and television. The western isles of Scotland were the only area in Scotland to retain the old faith of Roman Catholicism until today. This also might mean that more of the old myths were preserved. In the Presbyterian areas there has been a near complete destruction of anything Satanic or Romish. Many accounts of Scotland have come down to us

from Renaissance and latter travelers such as Donald
Muro and Daniel Defoe.

## 4. NORTHERN EUROPEAN DEVELOPMENT AND A NEW CONCEPT OF HUMAN NATURE

The building of Callanish implies a certain
theory of human nature. One that man has innate spatial,
mathematical and pattern recognition abilities that show
up before record keeping history and the city. Piaget
maintains that our conceptual structures exist and
function before language is learned by children. This
would mean that there would be no difficulty in terms of
understanding patterns in a culturally meaningful
manner. In a book on the development of
prehistoric art, symbols and astronomical
notation, Alexander Marshak comments on his
presupposition that prehistoric man would use lunar
movements to gauge time. He says:

Why then should he have kept a lunar notation?
Here we return to our prior assumptions. Against the

37

phases of the moon he told a story, or he told many stories. And against the phases of the moon he held at least some of his rites and ceremonies, which is another way of telling a story. And against the phases of the moon he structured his practical, social, cultural and biological life." (Marshak, 1972,136)

Thom does link the Callanish site with lunar movements. The people that built Callanish and their descendents seem to have been illiterate until the 19th century. This would mean that any myths would have been preserved for over 3.5 millennia. Almost all mythic structures would have been preserved through oral traditions. The construction and use of this site at the edge of the world means that literacy and urban populations are not necessary for what we today see as the formation of advanced conceptions of the world. If Plutarche's quote has some essence of truth then the Celts on the edge of the world, in the outer edges knew Saturn's orbit to be 29 years. This was seen on the shores of the world lake as a ridiculous supposition. The quote also has been interpreted as implying that these Hyboreans believed the solar system to be heliocentric. They developed all of these monuments without the city. Contemporary theories of societies and culture usually have some human nature based assumptions that development is inherent in that it must occur and that a definable linear track must be followed. If some of my deductions about the ramifications of Callanish are correct, then the entire conception that we hold about human nature and human societies are incorrect. As it is today, we rely too heavily on literacy in the wrong manner as a benchmark to the complexity and adaptation of a society. At the monastery of Iona, one of the nuclear points for the Christian reconversion of Europe during the early Medieval period literacy was a very rare occurrence. The men from this island, it ought to be noted and in Ireland were the most educated people in Europe. They were, even though they were illiterate.

The amount of prehistoric and protohistoric travel and cultural diffusion that occurred has always been underrated. In terms of the bronze age in Europe.

Cornwall, South England was the major source of tin. This means that from an early point the geographically isolated Western Isles of Europe were in trade contact with the Mediterranean Sea. The Semitic Mediterranean Sea peoples traded with the peoples of the Orkneys and Northern Scotland for furs and walrus tusks. There was contact between the Mediterranean civilizations and the people of Scotland.

## 5. FOLK CUSTOMS AND FOLK TALES AND THEIR RELATIONSHIP TO CALLANISH

Aubrey Burl refers back to a 19th century antiquarian who said people went to the stones secretly on May 1st and Midsummer. Previously, they had gone openly, but the Minister had forbidden all that. He also referred to a legend that when the sun rose on midsummer morning "something" came to the stone walking down the great avenue heralded by the call of the cuckoo bird, which is the traditional harbinger of Spring. An aside, but still might have some import is William Wordsworth's, the English 19th century nature poet, in "The Solitary Reaper" writes:

> A voice so thrilling was never heard,
> In spring-time from the Cuckoo bird,
>  Breaking the silence of the seas
> Among the farthest Hebrides.

Swire, in 1966, mentions a legend about Callanish that tells of a great priest-king, adorned with Mallard feathers, who came to the Isle of Lewis with many ships and had the stones erected by black slaves, many of whom died.

Robert L. Stevenson refers in "Heather Ale" to the "small dwarfish folk", who came before the Scots.

In a poem in 1749, William Collins, in his poem, "Ode on the Popular Superstition of the Highlands of Scotland", refers to the discovery of a vaulted chamber, on the island of Benbecula in the Hebrides that contained the bones of pygmies:

> Round the moist marge of each cold Hebrid isle,

To that hoar pile which still its ruin shows:
In whose small vaults a pigmy-folk is found,
Whose bones the delver with his spade upthrows,
And culls them, wond'ring, from the hallow'd ground:
Or thither where beneath the show'ry west.
The mighty kings of three fair realms are laid.

# 6. POTENTIAL RELATIONSHIPS WITH OTHER MEGALITHIC SITES

It is my opinion, as of now unproven, that there is some greater spatially defined structure through which these sites formed a larger shape on the landscape. Thom has maintained that the various monuments were produced by the same culture group and in many cases for the same reason. The sites on Lewis interrelate spatially for some purpose. Up to now, the site has been looked at in isolation. If I was able to, I would look at it in the context with other sites as a series of simultaneous observation points or a greater symbol which can only be seen aerially.

Thom does maintain that the various other sites and Callanish were for Lunar calendars.

## 7. PLACE-NAMES OF THE SITE

A short look at some of the place-names on the isle of Lewis might indicate in a general sense the past of the area. It is obvious from the few place-names that I looked up that the Norse invasions around 1000 A.D. affected the place-name structures of the area. This might mean that there was a near total extermination of the antecedent culture of the area. An example of this is the onomastic derivation of 'Callernish', "Callernish (W. of Lewis), like Kjalarnes, Iceland, 'keel cape'. Cf. Calava." (Johnston, 1970, p.122)

The derivation shows the name Callernish is related to a Norse settlement place-name and cannot be related to its previous gaelic and the name antecedent to its unknown gaelic name. The name Callernish is related to the place-name 'Calava Bay' in Sutherland. The nautical nature of both names is from the 'keel cape'. The keel is the bottom center beam of a ship from prow to

43

stern. Both Callernish and Calava Bay are related to the Old Norse word Kjala -meaning keel. The reference in The place-Names of Scotland for Calava Bay is, "Calava Bay (Sutherland) Tautology. 0. N. Kjala-r vag-r, 'keel bay' cf Calabost, Lewis; see p. 42" (Johnston, 1970, 121)

I was unable to find a reference to either the gaelic name, Tursachan (Callender, 1857, 381) or the other spelling of the site, Callanish. I have been unable to find the spelling of Callernish used by Martin in the first direct reference to the site, I have found referred to in other works. The spelling seems to have been standardized by 1857 when Callander first referred to it.

The derivation of the Isle of Lewis itself might refer to the pre-Old Norse place-name of the island. The old Norse name might indicate the Callernish site, it could be interpreted as a house. Also one might maintain that the site could be called silent and melancholy. Also the site could be maintained to be a house of song in reference to the legend that the cuckoo is supposed to walk down the concourse of the circle at certain times of the year singing. The reference in The Place-Names of Scotland is,

Lewis. A. 1100 Gael. M.S. Leodus, Sagas Lyoohus, c. 1225 Orkn. Sag. Liodhus, 1292 Lodoux, 1449 Leoghuis, 1580- gus. Perh. O.N. hljoo-r hus, 'silent, melancholy house', or as in sagas, Ijoo-hus, 'house of sone'. Many think carrup of G. Conig, 'a marsh', leogus-ghuis, 'marshiness'; appropriate enough but not agreeing with earliest forms."

(Johnston, 1970,p.239)

The site in prehistoric times is the most prominent cultural feature on the isle of Lewis and might have had some connection with the modern name of the island. The people themselves might have been the source of the songs. The site might have had rituals associated with song. It could have also had what is known today as Scottish mouth music. My conclusions from looking at the place-names are ambiguous with those tantalizing glimpses at what might be behind the place-names.

## 8. POSSIBLE FOOD ECONOMIES

Before the extensive over hunting of whales during the last two hundred years whales would have been part of the potential food resources of the people of the Hebrides. Again I have been unable to find any reference to prehistoric whale hunting in the Hebrides or on the west coast of Scotland. Any ancient peoples would have an obvious marine orientation so the logiclal result would be that they would have th expertise to hunt whales in the fjords and straits on the west coast. The marine orientation might be a catalyst to the advancement of astronomical knowledge in antiquity. Seafaring nations have the need of knowledge of the heavens to guide short and long voyages. They also become more attuned to the forces of marine nature. This would suggest the contention by Thom that there was some type of use of Calernish to measure annual degeneration and regeneration of the climate.

I have not come across any reference to the use of fish as fertilizer in the Outer Hebrides. This use of fish to increase productivity would allow for increased productivity and the attendant potentially larger population. It is only pure conjecture as to the relationship between marine products and agriculture.

From general reading, a uniquee agricultural technique was practiced on the Western coast of Scotland back into antiquity. This practice was the use of seaweed as a crop fertilizer. This practice alone increases crop fertilitysubstantially. Seaweed is very common in the waters of the Hebrides. If this practice was used along with other techniques potential agricultural production could support a relatively large population. There have been many historical examples of

47

agricultural techniques being completely forgotten or being downgraded. To substantiate this one only has to look at modern agriculture and the amount of lost knowledge on the nature of proper agricultural techniques.

I have found no reference to my conjecture that the dependence on marine and freshwater marine was larger than has been maintained. The salmon runs on the west coast of Scotland and in the Outer Hebrides is to-day of a comparable volume to the North American North-West coast salmon runs.

Salmon in such plenty as is scarcely credible, and so cheap, that to those who have any substance to buy with, it is not worth their while to catch it themselves. This they eat fresh in the season and for other times they cure it by drying it in the sun, by which they preserve it all the year.

(Defoe, 1962, Vol. 2, p.494)

The reliance upon marine resources was greater than is stated today. Fish could also mean the development of a culture with a stable leisured class which in turn could develop an astronomy independently.

## 9. THE PALAEOENVIRONMENT OF THE ISLE OF LEWIS

From my general readings previous to this course and the specific materials I have collected for this paper that the present climate is not the same climate that existed during the time of the building of the megalithic site, Callernish was built. My private contention is that the site proves this along with some reasons behind the formation of peat on the Isle of Lewis.

That major climatic shifts occurred during the past in the Gaellic islands, has been a widely accepted contention for the past two and a half centuries. In a natural history published in 1726 there was reference to the possibility that climate shifts had happened in the past. This was in the context that several feet of peat that had formed in bogs over formerly plowed fields. The Archbishop in 1726 wrote,

This certain Ireland has been better inhabited than it is at present; mountains that now are covered with boggs have formerly been plowed: for when you dig five or six foot deep, you discover a proper soil for vegetable and find it plowed into ridges and furrows...

(Herity and Eogan, 1977, p.250 (King , in Molneus, 1726, p.163)

This early work does state an interpretation that might or might not be correct. It is interesting that such an interpretation was made at this early point.

Other more contemporary works attempt to prove that major shifts did not occur in the period of 4500 B.0 to present. Reference to analysis of Oxygen 016/018 isotope ratios in the Greenland ice cap strata cores is externally and internally conflicting.

These isotope ratios were originally intended only to indicate macro-climate shifts such as the Pleistocene/ Holocene boundary and the attendant global climate shifts. In The Environment in British Prehistory the common mistake of using th ice cap oxygen isotopes to regional and micro-climate occurs,

Evidence for cyclical fluctuations of climate, however, is now very considerable, as illustrated for instance by the oxygen isotope work (Simmons and Tooley, 1981, p.143).

The discussion of oxygen isotopes as a gauge of non mega climate shifts, as is done in reference to British prehistory, is ridiculous.

The site of Callanish is supposed to have had several feet of a peat bog that accumulated around and partially buried the bottom portion of the stones. The question of whether climate shifts did occur directly affects the formation of the overburden of peat at this site and at other sites. It is my contention that the regional climate of this area during prehistory has been misrepresented. This in turn would affect the food surplus, potential population, the ease of existence and the formation of a leisured class. As it is today, palm trees grow in Uig which is rather interesting noting the fact that Uig is at such a northern latitude.

Peat bogs stratify according to humid/non-'humid periods contemporary to the strata formation. The different peat strata are differentiated by variations between light brown to black. These different strata have been attributed to increased humidity, followed by increased precipitation and standing surface water accumulation. On the horizons of the light strata there is an increase of density of pollen. When the Western isles of Europe were first occupied they were, according to pollen analysis, thickly forested. One theorem of peat formation contends that it only occurred in podzolic soils with a humid marine climate. It says that peat formation starting is an indicator of the clearance of the former forest. This, it seems, was usually done by fire. I found no reference to potential slash and burn agriculture in Scotland. It is my opinion that there was an adapted form of slash and burn agriculture that eventually destroyed the ecological equilibrium of the island. This would have resulted from the slash and burn cycle becoming too short for an adequate rejuvenation of the soil's fertility. This resulted in a complete ecological disruption. The ultimate result is the heaths, which in reality are 'wastelands'. On the other hand this ecological collapse might also have linked with one of the hypothesized cyclical declines of North Atlantic climate.

If there were a dramatic increase in humidity and/or precipitation then this would, at least partly, explain why an ancient astronomical observatory would have been built in an area that is now almost continually obscured by mist, fogs, and clouds. This increase in precipitation might also explain why peat formation occurred after Callernish w built. Six feet of peat in approximately 3600 years is quite a lot of growth. The very astronomical nature of Callanish indicates the different climate that was in existence when it was built. This was pointed out by Captain Somerville in1912.

So elaborate a science as astrology, if it can be proved to exist, could scarcely spring up spontaneously among a barbarous people; and in our cloudy climate would be unlikely to rise at all; the heavenly bodies being so rarely capable of continuous observation: unless, indeed, the meteorological conditions of 4,000 years ago were extremely different from those of today. If it is th case

that such a cult once existed in these climates, we must,
I think, look to a sunnier, less humid country than our
own; such as that East, whence the British religion of
today has sprung as the place of origin for that of
prehistori days in these islands.

(Somerville, 1912, p.51)

Somerville felt that it was impossible for
such a monument and the astronomical
knowledge obviously behind it to have originated in
the Hebrides. He does, also, point out the logical
deduction that the atmospheric conditions must
have been dramatically clearer when the main portion
of Callernish was built. This observation might fit
into the increased humidity that was necessary for
peat formation.

This original deduction by Somerville is, in my
opinion, a necessary part of a new and greater

understanding of Callanish's position in the prehistory of the Western isles of Europe.

# THE VIKINGS IN NORTH AMERICA:

# A PRELIMINARY STUDY OF THE NORSE GREENLAND COLONIES

# By:

# Austin A. Mardon

# Table of Contents

The Vikings have been receiving bad press for more than a thousand years. The early sea-bound expeditions of the inhabitants of the Scandinavian peninsula in the 9th Century were for plunder. They harassed foreign lands to the south and east. These Viking raiders were, in their day, as the Roman Legions were in the days of Julius Caesar, or the Spanish Conquestadors in the 16th Century.

In the beginning, they pillaged and burned, but later, they settled down in new lands to become farmers, fishermen or merchant, and many were able administrators, good soldiers and skilled craftsmen.

Where did the Vikings or Norse come from? They came from the fjords of Norway or the flat lands of Denmark. We know there was a sudden as yet unexplained population growth. Many a younger son decided to leave their homeland to seek their fortune across the seas. The Vikings were the most skilful ship builders in Europe at this time. Their 'long-boat' powered either by a square woolen sail or rows of hardy oarsmen, ventured out across the North Atlantic Ocean. They were practical navigators.

## I. SOURCES OF OUR INFORMATION CONCERNING THE VIKINGS IN NORTH AMERICA

There are three main sources of information concerning the Vikings and their visits to North America from the well-established 400-year old Greenland colonies. Sometimes they support one another, and sometimes they provide apparently conflicting pieces of evidence. The first source is the wealth of archaeological remains dating from the 10th Century. For centuries, and as a result of ever-improving modern techniques, particularly in recent times, professional and amateur archaeologists have discovered Viking ruins, tools and weapons in Greenland, the Canadian Arctic Islands, and the North Eastern Seaboard of the North American continent.

Possibly, the most significant ruin was at the Norse settlement site at L' Anse aux Meadows, in Northern Newfoundland near Belle Isle Strait. Scholars and archaeologists only located this site, consisting of three groups of houses or different farm steadings on the shore of Black Duck Brook in 1960. The houses were made of turf, and many artifacts, including a spindle whorl, have been found. The presence of the L' Ause aux Meadow spindle whorl appears to indicate that there were women in the settlement that remained for several years in this locality. Also found at this site are bronze ring pins, similar to those found in Norse settlements in Iceland, Hebrides and Ireland in the late mediaeval period.

Another recent archaeological find is a fragment of chain mail woolen cloth, iron rivets, fragments of coopered barrels and pieces of iron and copper from a Thule Eskimo site on Ellesmere Island in the high Canadian Arctic. This might indicate contact between the Norse and Eskimos were more frequent and more extensive than European historical accounts record.

A series of radiocarbon tests dating this Eskimo winter house range from the 10th to the 15th century, but the average date is the mid-13th century. (Gordon, 1981)

It is now accepted that when the Norse colonies in Greenland was thriving, the weather was much warmer than it is today. It is possible that vessels could and did circumnavigate Greenland.

These Norse artifacts would have found their way to the site they were found, by Eskimos bring them there, Eskimos recovering them from a wrecked Norse ship, or after killing a Norse raiding party, or final from a Norse temporary settlement.

Of such finds as L' Anse aux Meadow or Thule reconfirm, or put into prospective, from surviving written records contained the sagas.

## 2. THE SAGAS

The Icelandic Sagas or prose narratives, describing the early history of the Norse settlements in Iceland with lists of 3,000 names of the original pioneer settlers, were written down for the first time in the 12th century. The Icelandic word "Saga" means "what is said or told." They are derived from both folk tales and oral traditions of historical events. Today, most scholars recognize that in many cases the personages and facts are of real people and factually correct. The Sagas are a unique record of the life and times, habits, laws, and customs of this group of Norse folk.

There are some thirty Icelandic Sagas that have survived from the late Medieval time.

The Greenlanders' Saga narrates how Bjarni who had been forced off course on a trip from Iceland to Greenland and apparently reached landfall somewhere along the wooded coast of Labrador. He then sailed north until he sighted either the Torngat Mountain region of northern Labrador or Baffin Island.

Later Leif Ericson, the son of Eric the Red, founder of the Greenland colonies, sailed west, naming the land he discovered Markland (Woodland?) and Vinland. It is accepted as fact that Leif Ericson discovered, landed, explored and attempted to make a permanent settlement on the northeast coast of Continental North America. The exact location is still to be discovered by archaeologists.

## 3. THE THIRD SOURCE OF INFORMATION: OTHER WRITTEN RECORDS

The first surviving written record that mentioned "Vinland" by name is found in Adam of Bremen's History of the Archbisop of Hamburgh, written in about 1075.

Book Four of this history is entitled "A Description of the Islands of the North" and in it, Adam of Breman declares "The King" (Svein of Denmark spoke to me) "about yet another island which had been discovered by many in the ocean (West of Greenland). It is called Vinland because there grow wild in that country vines which produce fine wine. Free-growing crops abound there. I have learned this not from fanciful tales but from the trust worth reports of the Danes" (Quoted by Logan, 1983) Other pre-Saga references to the existence of Vinland, include Albertus Magnus, the medieval geographer.

The Icelandic Annuals of the year 1121 record that "Bishop Erric of Greenland set out in search of Vinland." There is no entry saying that he found it or had returned safely. (Gordon, 1981); while The Icelandic Annuals of the year 1347 states that a ship on a voyage to Marland was blown by a storm eastward to Iceland.

The problem about consulting the Sagas directly is partly due to indifferent translations from the original medieval Icelandic. It would be a great service if a knowledgeable Icelandic linguistic scholar was to prepare a careful annotated edition of certain key passages of the Sagas, dealing with Leif Ericson's journey to Vinland. As Kate Gordon observes a case for location of Leif's colony are diverse as Labrador, Florida, the Great Lakes on the Hudson Bay.

## 4. GREENLAND

Greenland is almost two-hundred miles due west of Iceland. But the mountains are so high on both islands that half-way across one can still see the Snaefellsness in Iceland in the east and the summits of Angmassalik in Greenland to the west.

According to tradition, it was about 900 A.D. that the existence of Greenland was know, but it was some three generations later that Eric the Red led an expedition from Iceland. The east coast of Greenland, like the east coast of Iceland was inhospitable for settlement. He established his colony at the head of Tunugliafic fjord and named it after the fertile land, lush with grass, he found there.

Ten years later, he established another colony further north up the west coast of Greenland, which he called "Godshaven." It is opposite Baffin Island.

The mild climate in the Medieval period made it possible for the Greenlanders to grow corn, but animal husbandry was the main resource. Lack of any timber was a problem, and had to be imported from "Markland" on the other side of the Davis Strait.

Archaeological evidence reveals that cattle, sheep, goats and pigs were reared in large numbers. The European demand for walrus ivory and polar-bear skins resulted in the export of these in exchange for corn and much needed iron. The fishermen of the colony caught whale, seal and a large quantity of fish.

Archaeologists have declared the coffins at Herjulfsnes are made of large planks of pine, deal and larch, and the larch certainly cannot have come all the long sea voyage from Norway. It is reasonable to conclude that wood was being imported from Markland for most of the life of the Greenland colonies.

## 5. NOTES ON RELIGIOUS HISTORY OF GREENLAND COLONIES

In the 11th Century, Greenlands' settlements were part of the archbishopric of Hamburg as was all of

Scandinavia and the areas conquered by the Norse including Isle of Man, Hebrides, Shellands Orkneys and Iceland.

In the 1150's, Nicholas Brekspeare, an English-born papal ambassador, established the archbishopric of Nidaros (the present Trondheim) in Northern Norway, Greenland was transferred from the jurisdiction of Hamburg to that of Nidaros. From 1152 most of the relations between the Vatican and Greenland were through the archbishops of Nidaros.

The first bishop of Greenland was Eric Gnupsson who was a crusader in his youth. The last surviving written reference to bishop Gnupsson was in 1121 when he set out to convert the inhabitants of "Vinland." There is no record of him surviving this missionary journey.

In 1124, his successor Arnold was consecrated bishop of Gardar, Greenland. In 1152, he was transferred to Hameren in Norway and died there. From Adam of Breman, we learn the inhabitants of the two Greenland settlements were under the jurisdiction of the bishop-polatinate as their overlord. To our knowledge, there were nineteen Greenland churches. In the eastern settlement, the Cathedral ruins at Bardar is located and is dedicated to Saint Nicholas. The Churches of an Augustinian monastery and a Benedictine convent have also been found. The Greenland churches appear to have been built under the influence of Irish ecclesiastical architecture.

Vatican records reveal that several Popes were concerned and insistent on the payment of taxes to assist the crusades and also for correct doctrine and proper sacramental practices. Vilhjalmur stefansson in Greenland (1942) maintains that the population of Greenland was around 8,000 or 10,000 in the 13th century. The religious fervor as indicated by the building of large stone churches was greater among the Greenlanders than in Iceland with more than five times the population. The Gardar Cathedral was 75 feet in length while the best preserved church, built at Hvalsejarfjord, is 52 feet long and 26 feet wide with walls from four to five feet thick still standing to the height of thirteen feet. The churches face east so the Gospel can be preached into the pagan north where the Eskimos (skraellings) dwelt. During the singing or praying of the Creed, the Greenlanders use to draw their swords and hold them aloft.

Archeological investigations of Greenland graves reveal that devotion to Virgin May was widespread. It is usual in the excavation of graves that wooden crosses are discovered carved with devout runes; most frequent of all references to the Virgin (This may be an indication that the Kensington Stone carver may have been a Greenlander).

## 6. THE WANING OF THE GREENLAND SETTLEMENTS

Greenland has been always recognized as being part of North America. Iceland, on the other hand, has been included in Europe. After four hundred years, did thousands of devout Christians one day just walk into the sea in a lemming-like migration?

The Catholic faith appears to have taken strong root in the two settlements. If so, it would be doubtful if they would after generations of warring with the Skraellings, suddenly join up with them. It does not appear that the colonies were overrun and destroyed quickly by a sudden invasion.

"Malnutrition school" supporters say that the Greenland Colonies were permanently cut off from European shipping in the 14th century and they became extinct through two main courses: First malnutrition from lack of imported grains and vegetables, and second attacks on the weakened population by Eskimos.

In support of the malnutrition position Dr. Poul Norland at Herjolfsness in 1921 exumed skeletons. Several of the remains of ricket victims were dug-up north of the Church building, the traditional burial ground of paupers.

As a historical geographer, I am well aware that the hunter/gather in a neolithic cultural stage such as the Greenland Eskimos, might appear to have a lower evolutionary status than the farmer/fisherman Norse Greenlanders.

However, when the climate commenced getting colder, the farmers may be forced to become hunters and nomadic rather than sedentary. Could this have happened in the Greenland Colonies?

In 1885, Richard Jefferies wrote After London, which describes England after a collapse into barbarism and such a scenario is possibly what happened in Greenland in the late middle ages. Wilert Sundt, the 19th Century Norwegian sociologist and historian, in Egedes Dagbog i Udtaq states that the Greenlanders had a population with higher education, Christian and relatively civilized, would fall so low and disappear in mixing with a crude race (Inuit). But that a population like the Norse in Greenland, which had been living there 400 years, should disappear completely is just as rare an occurrence (See: Stefansson Greenland

(1942), pp 179□ 181). He believed the Norse Greenlanders disappeared by amalgamation rather than by extermination after there was a climatic change for the worse.

FOOTNOTES:

1. Personal observation: Some 33 years ago, my father came to Canada from Britain and wrote an article while a reporter that the area visited was in the Hudson Bay. He maintained that the geographical description of Vinland of the Sagas was closer to the lowlands of the Mouth of the Nelson river on the southern shore of the Hudson Bay than the rocky coast of Nova Scotia. He believed that was on the right track when he discovered several aging ballard holes along the Nelson River. However, on investigation, he was informed the moorings had been built in 1813 by Norwegian ex-prisoners □ of-war who had volunteered to row the Selkirk settlers up stream to Fort Garry.

BIBLIOGRAPHY

Gordon, Kate. The Vikings and Their Predecessors. Ottawa: National Museum of Man, National Museum of Canada, 1981.

Hermannsson, Halldor "The Problems of Wineland:" Islandica Vol. 25 Ithaca: Cornell University Press, 1936. (The footnotes in this interesting article contains a list of the significant works on the subject up t o that time: recommended reading)

Heyerdahl, Thor "Columbus and the Vikings" in Early Man and the Ocean. New York: Doubleday, 1979.

Logan, F. Donald The Viking in History. Totowa, N.J.: Barnes and Noble, 1983.

Morison, Samuel Eliot The European Discovery of America: The Northern Voyages AD 500-1600. New York, Oxford University Press, 1971. (The author states that the Kensington Stone is a 'clumsy forgery')

Stefansson, Vilhjalmur Greenland. New York: Doubleday, 1942.

## About the Author

Dr. Austin A. Mardon was born in Edmonton, the son of E.G. Mardon and May Mardon, an Edmonton teacher. Educated at Lethbridge, he did an M.A. at South Dakota State University and his Ph.D. at Greenwich University, Australia. He then served as a research scientist and participated in a meteorite recovery expedition in the late 1980's, spending some 50 days in a two-man tent 170 miles from the South Pole. He is a life member of the New York Explorer's Club.

His main work has been his humanitarian efforts with those suffering from schizophrenia and other mental illnesses. He has been active also with his father, Dr. Ernest G. Mardon, in authoring a score of books and academic articles, the latest of which is a series of historical studies of ethnic groups and Alberta politics. Dr. Mardon was appointed a member of the Order of Canada in 2007.

## About the Editor

Aala Abdullahi is currently a Neuroscience student at the University of Alberta in Edmonton, Alberta.

www.ingramcontent.com/pod-product-compliance
Lightning Source LLC
Chambersburg PA
CBHW021838020426

42334CB00014B/684